SCIENCE
COLORING BOOK!

DISCOVER AND ENJOY A VARIETY OF COLORING PAGES FOR KIDS

This is a Bleed-through page if you are using a coloring marker or pen!

Bold Illustrations

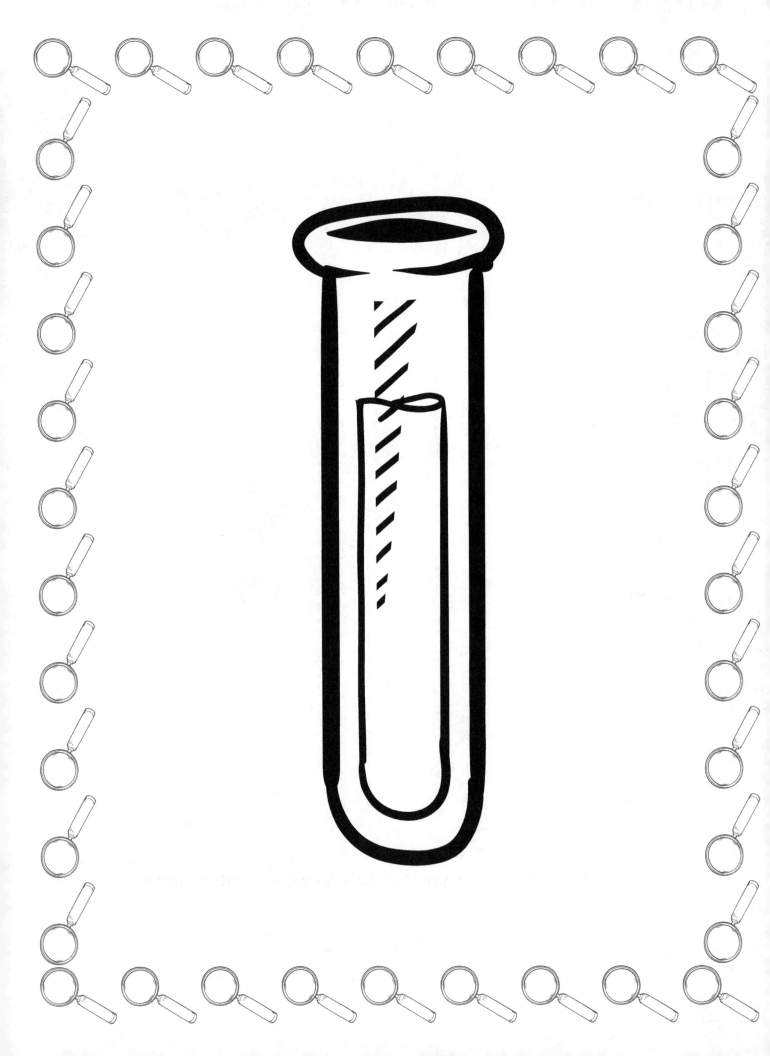

This is a Bleed-through page if you are using a coloring marker or pen!

Bold Illustrations

This is a Bleed-through page if you are using a coloring marker or pen!

Bold Illustrations

This is a Bleed-through page if you are using a coloring marker or pen!

Bold Illustrations

This is a Bleed-through page if you are using a coloring marker or pen!

Bold Illustrations

This is a Bleed-through page if you are using a coloring marker or pen!

Bold Illustrations

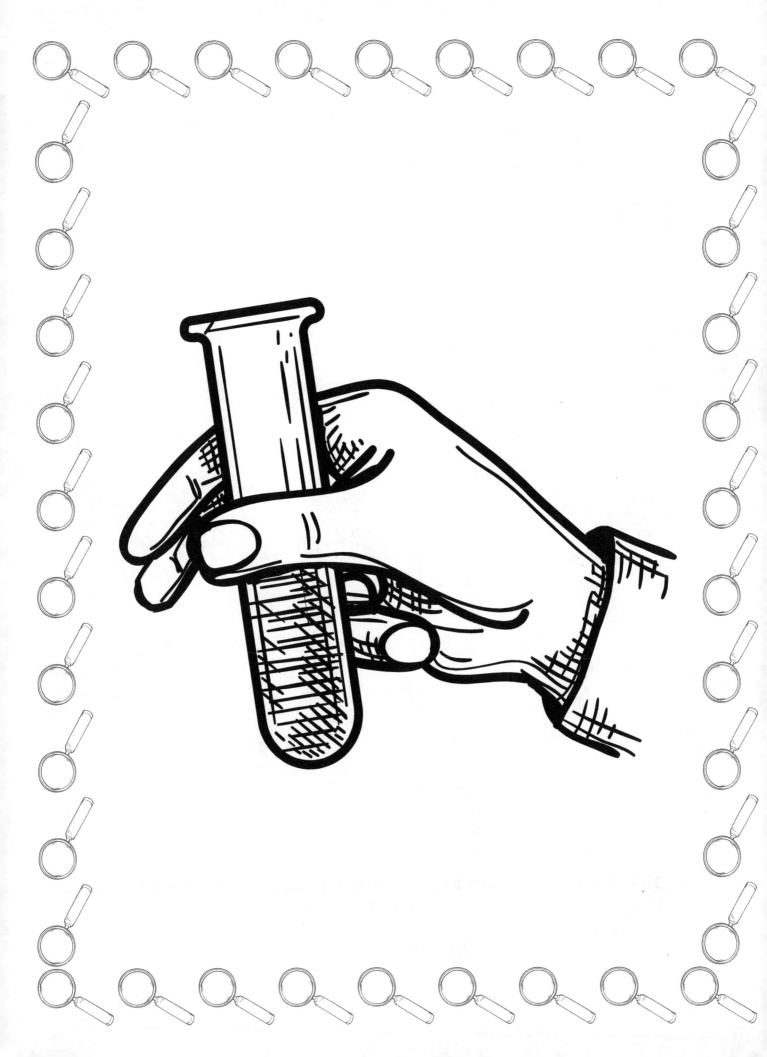

This is a Bleed-through page if you are using a coloring marker or pen!

Bold Illustrations

This is a Bleed-through page if you are using a coloring marker or pen!

Bold Illustrations

This is a Bleed-through page if you are using a coloring marker or pen!

Bold Illustrations

This is a Bleed-through page if you are using a coloring marker or pen!

Bold Illustrations

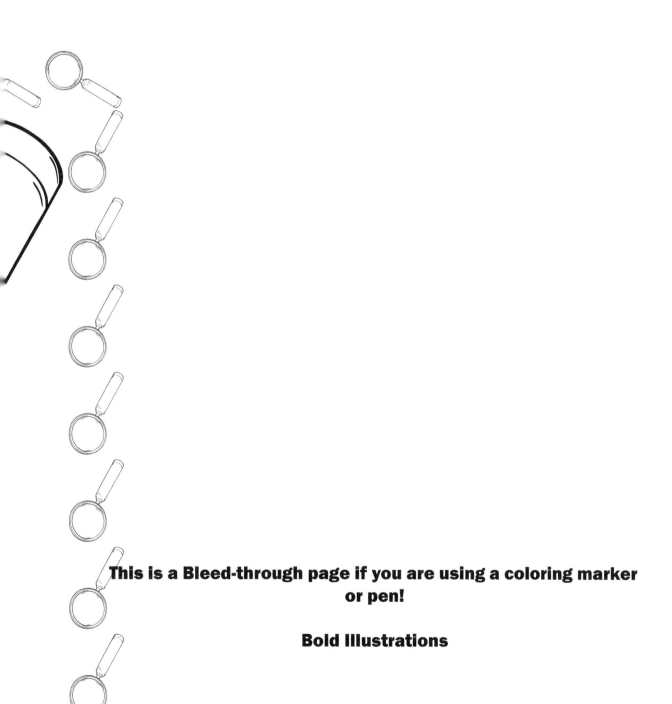

This is a Bleed-through page if you are using a coloring marker or pen!

Bold Illustrations

This is a Bleed-through page if you are using a coloring marker
or pen!

Bold Illustrations

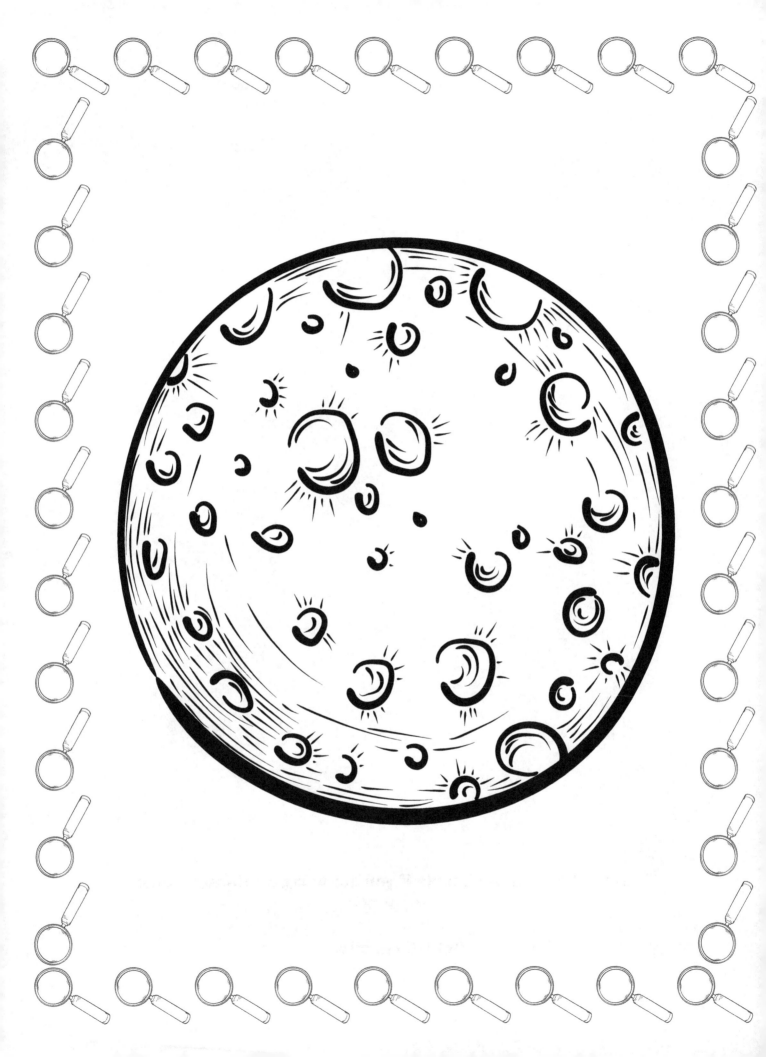

This is a Bleed-through page if you are using a coloring marker or pen!

Bold Illustrations

This is a Bleed-through page if you are using a coloring marker or pen!

Bold Illustrations

This is a Bleed-through page if you are using a coloring marker or pen!

Bold Illustrations

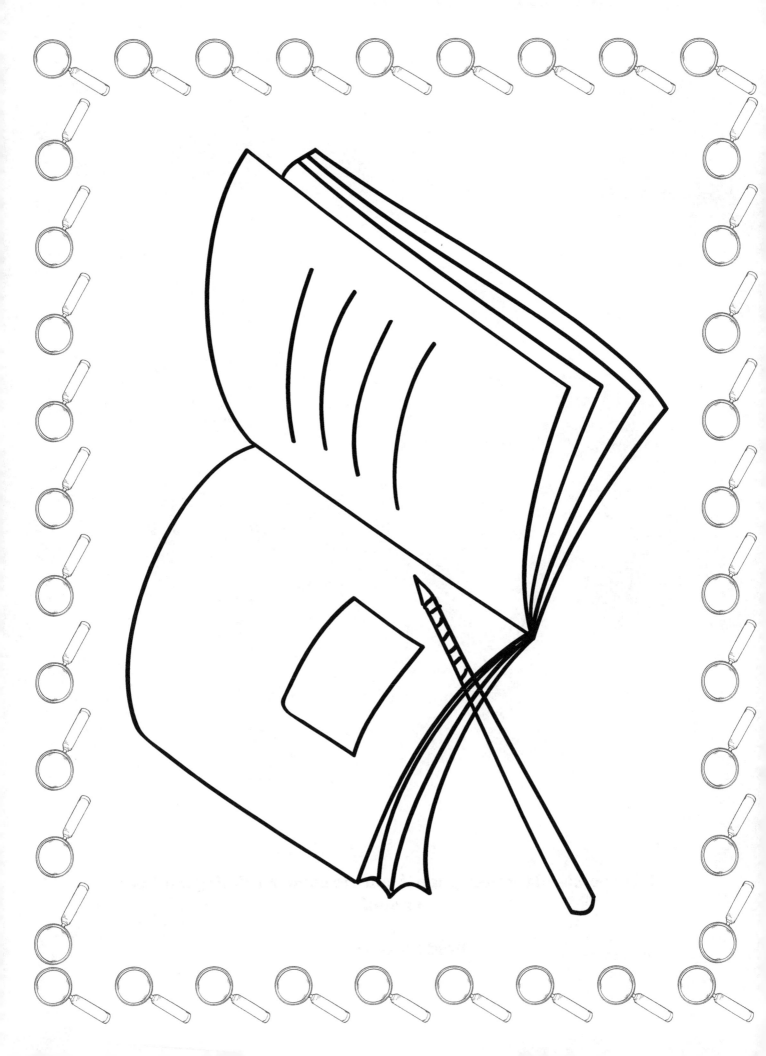

This is a Bleed-through page if you are using a coloring marker or pen!

Bold Illustrations

This is a Bleed-through page if you are using a coloring marker or pen!

Bold Illustrations

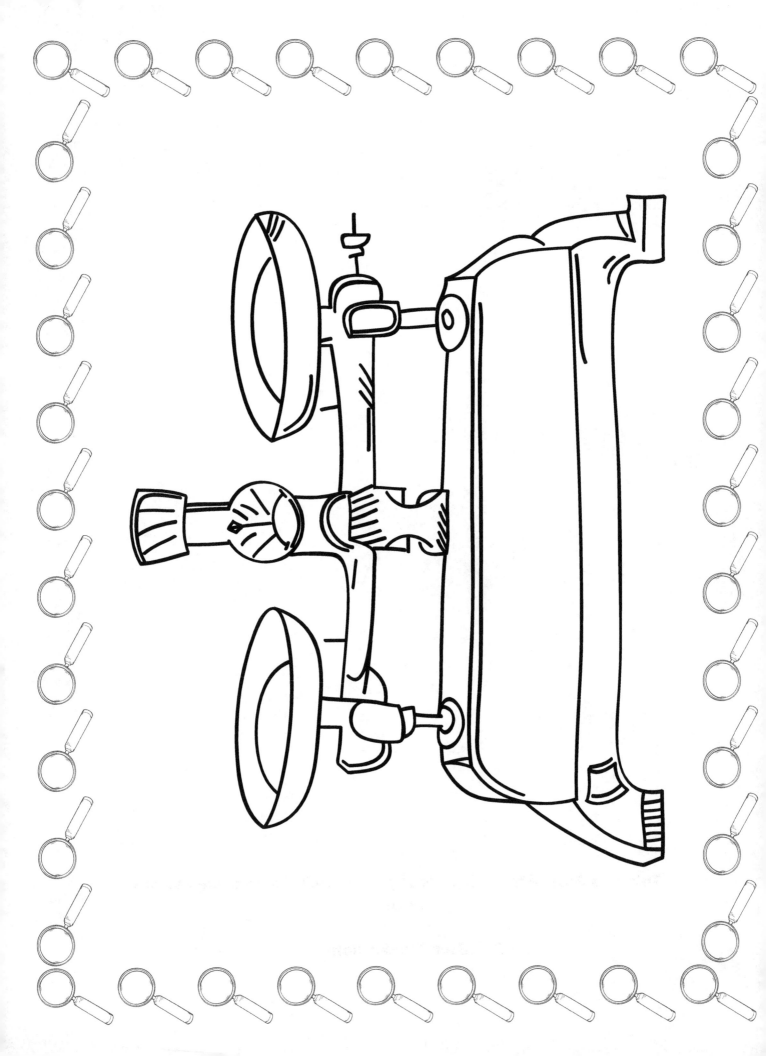

This is a Bleed-through page if you are using a coloring marker or pen!

Bold Illustrations

This is a Bleed-through page if you are using a coloring marker or pen!

Bold Illustrations

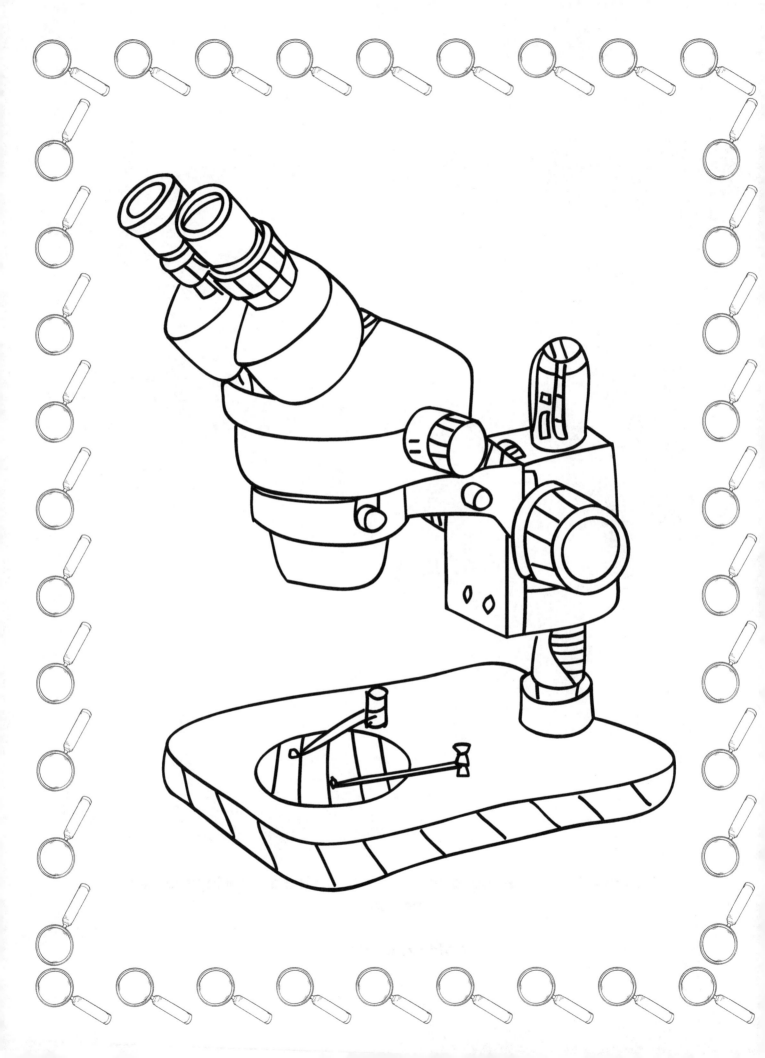

This is a Bleed-through page if you are using a coloring marker or pen!

Bold Illustrations

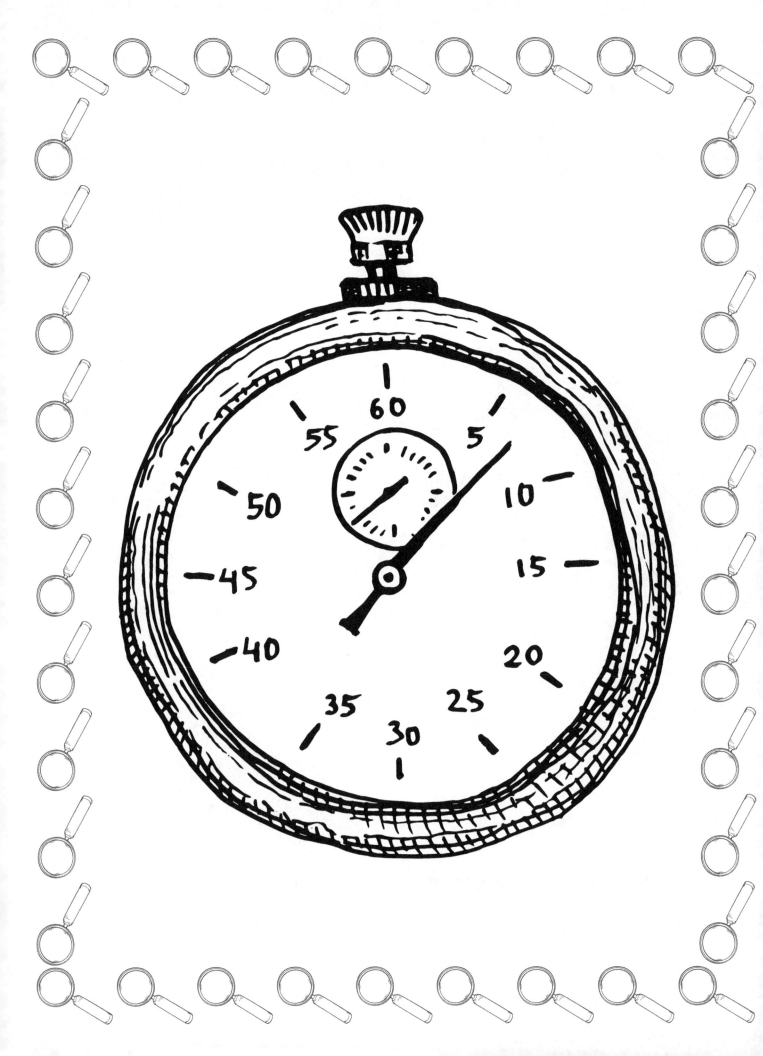

This is a Bleed-through page if you are using a coloring marker
or pen!

Bold Illustrations

This is a Bleed-through page if you are using a coloring marker or pen!

Bold Illustrations

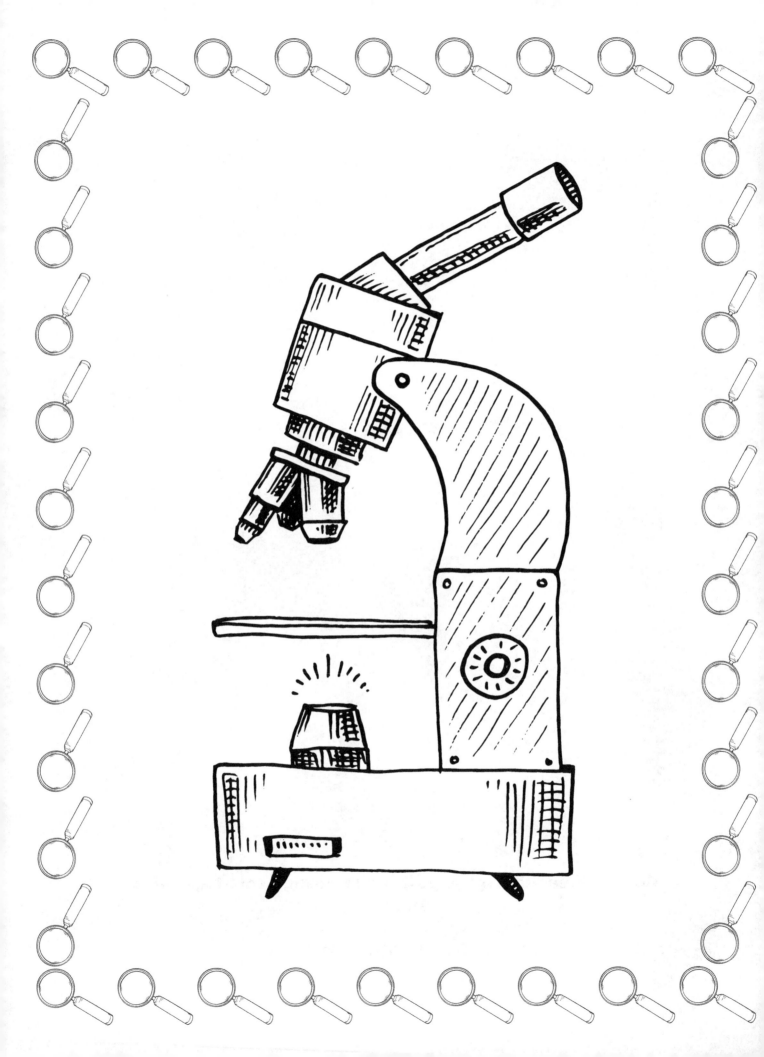

This is a Bleed-through page if you are using a coloring marker or pen!

Bold Illustrations

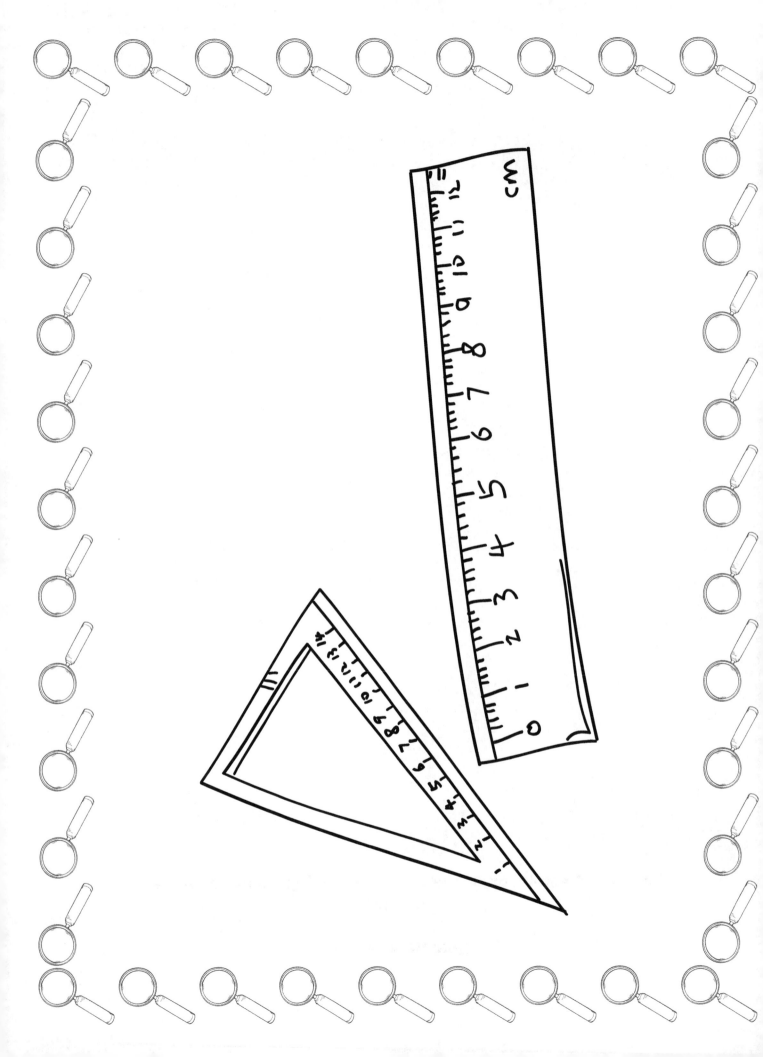

This is a Bleed-through page if you are using a coloring marker
or pen!

Bold Illustrations

This is a Bleed-through page if you are using a coloring marker or pen!

Bold Illustrations

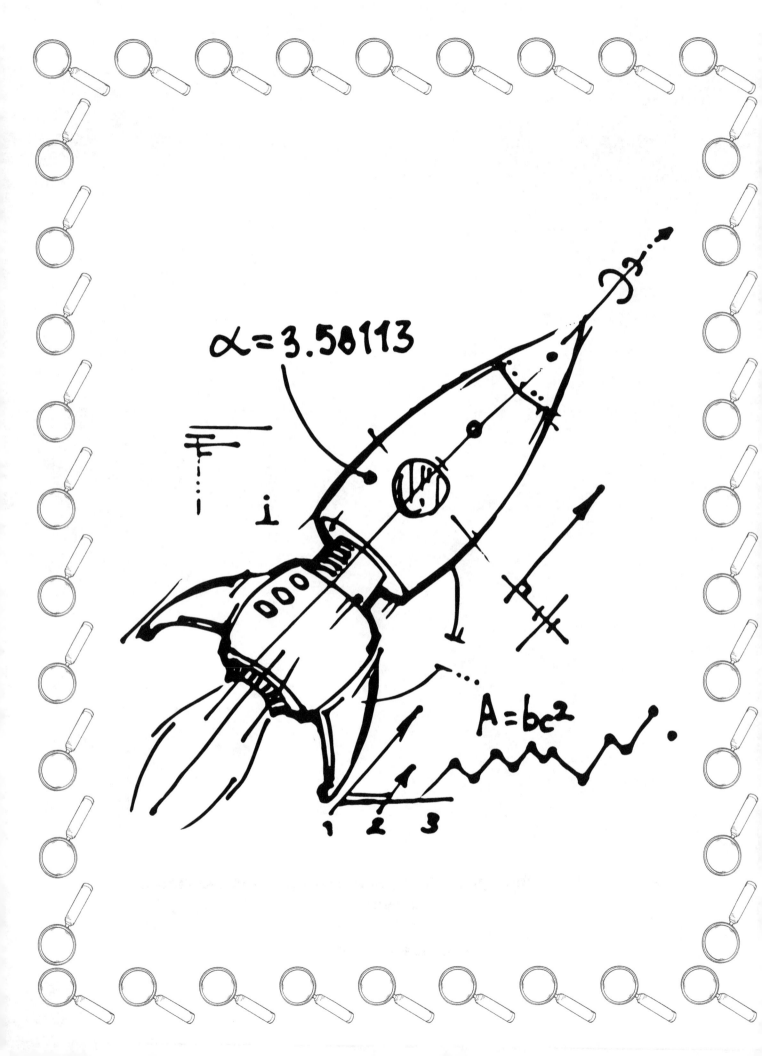

This is a Bleed-through page if you are using a coloring marker or pen!

Bold Illustrations

This is a Bleed-through page if you are using a coloring marker
or pen!

Bold Illustrations

This is a Bleed-through page if you are using a coloring marker or pen!

Bold Illustrations

This is a Bleed-through page if you are using a coloring marker or pen!

Bold Illustrations

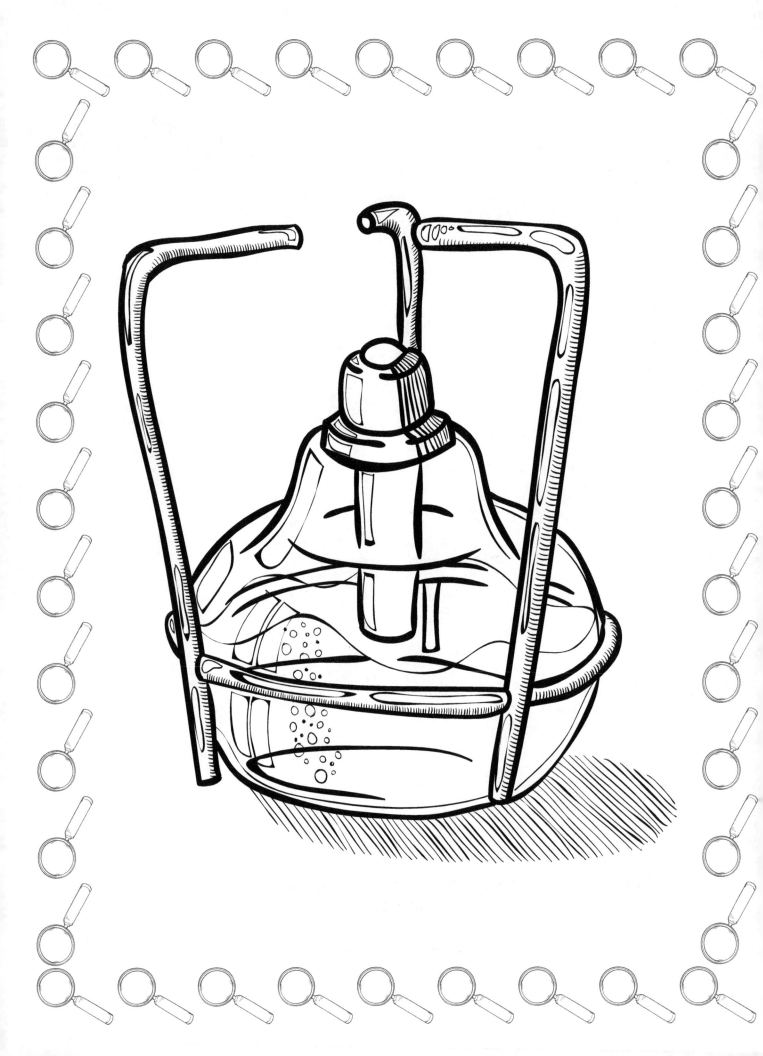

This is a Bleed-through page if you are using a coloring marker or pen!

Bold Illustrations

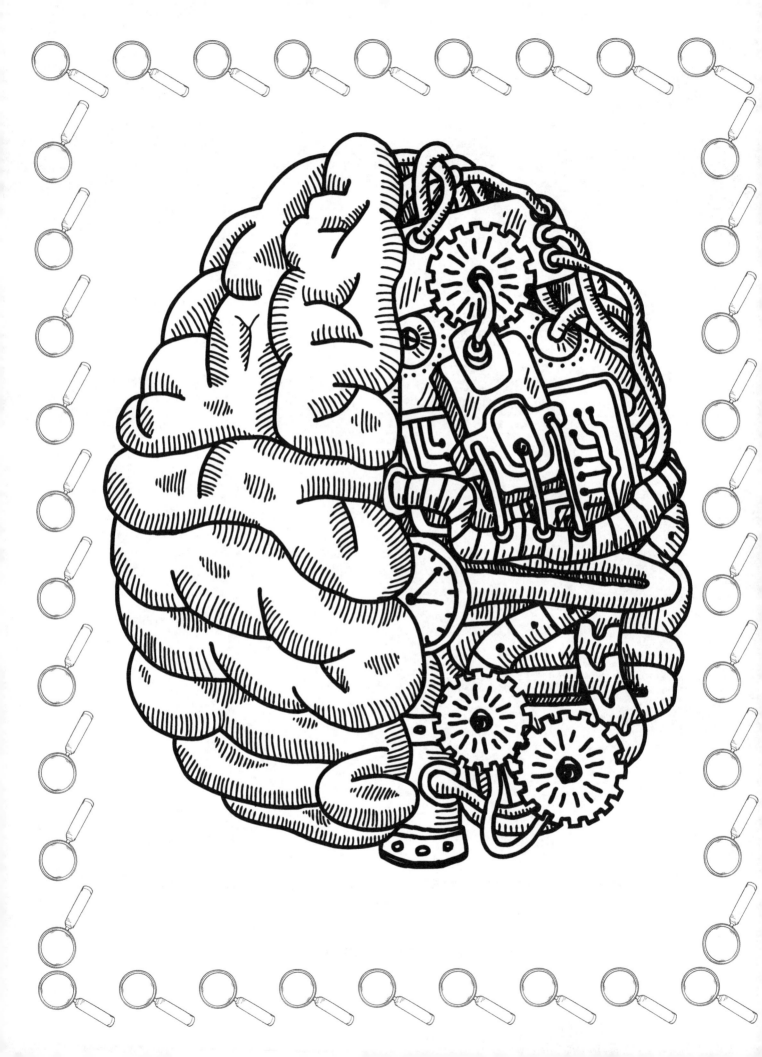

This is a Bleed-through page if you are using a coloring marker or pen!

Bold Illustrations

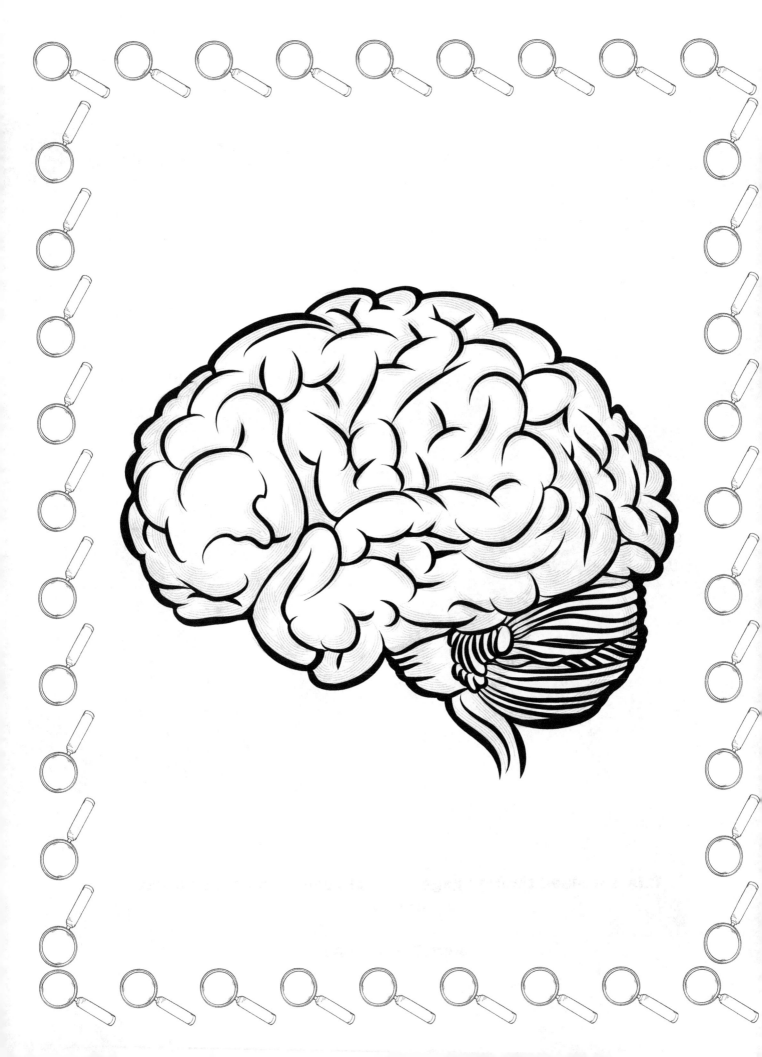

This is a Bleed-through page if you are using a coloring marker or pen!

Bold Illustrations

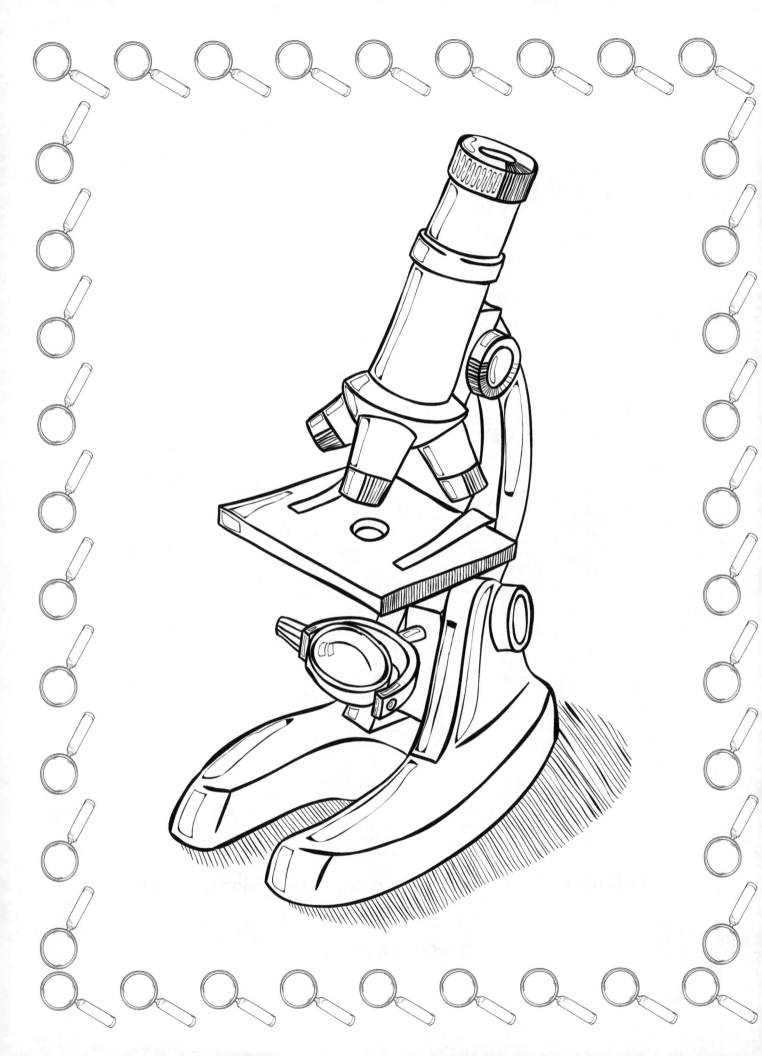

This is a Bleed-through page if you are using a coloring marker or pen!

Bold Illustrations

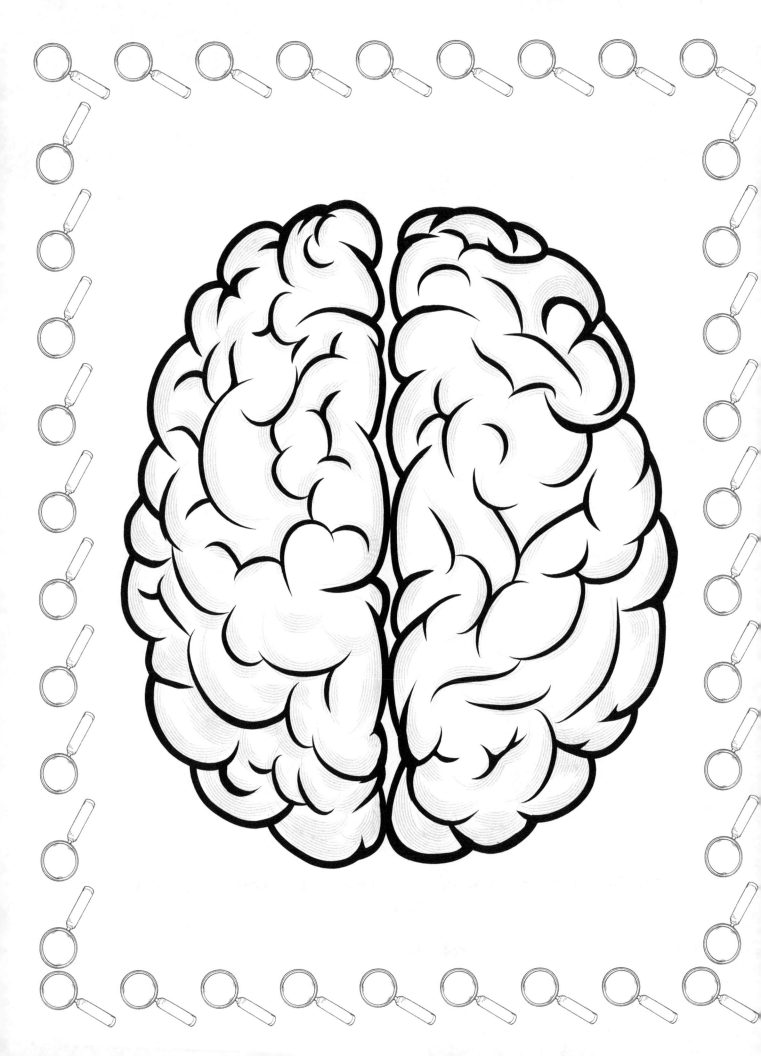

This is a Bleed-through page if you are using a coloring marker or pen!

Bold Illustrations

This is a Bleed-through page if you are using a coloring marker or pen!

Bold Illustrations

This is a Bleed-through page if you are using a coloring marker or pen!

Bold Illustrations

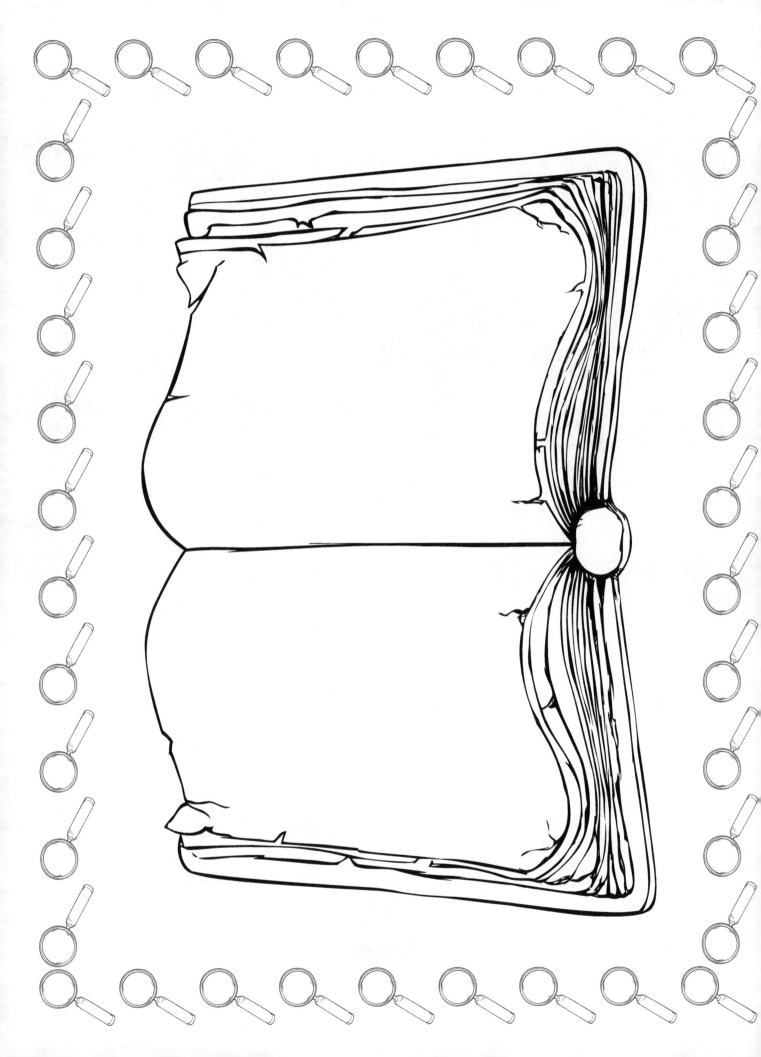

This is a Bleed-through page if you are using a coloring marker
or pen!

Bold Illustrations

This is a Bleed-through page if you are using a coloring marker or pen!

Bold Illustrations

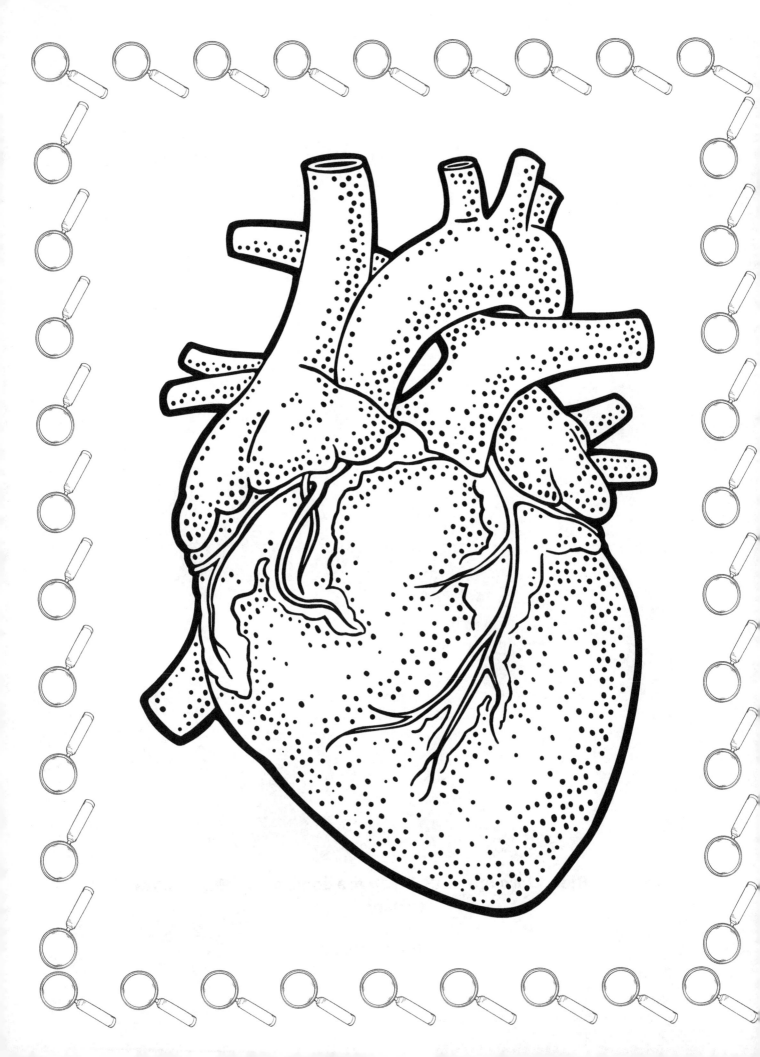

This is a Bleed-through page if you are using a coloring marker or pen!

Bold Illustrations

CPSIA information can be obtained
at www.ICGtesting.com
Printed in the USA
BVHW010047210821
614786BV00034B/556